Dedicated to:
Olivia, Bri, Luke, Joel, Cody & Kristine
My Focus Missionaries
&
St. Catherine of Siena Newman Center
Drake University

Written by: Abigail Gartland

Hello, my name is St. Catherine of Siena!

I was born in Italy in 1347.

I had a very large family growing up. I was the youngest of 25 kids!

When I was only 5 years old, I had a vision of Jesus.

In my vision, He was giving me a blessing.

A few years later, when I was 7 years old, I vowed to give my life to Jesus.

I wanted to keep my promise to Jesus, but when I was 17 years old, my parents wanted me to get married.

I told my parents that my wish in life was to be dedicated to Jesus, and not to marry a man.

My parents accepted my wishes, and I joined a sisterhood of the Dominican order.

I spent my first few years in complete silence, and only spent time with Jesus in prayer.

After a few years, I went out into the world to help others with their relationships to Jesus.

When I was 28 years old, I got the stigmata which means that I had the same wounds that Jesus did when He was nailed to the cross.

When I was 33 years old, I passed away, and went to be with Jesus in Heaven.

In 1970, I was made as a doctor of the church. Being a doctor of the church is one of the highest honors for a saint.

Being a doctor of the church means that I dedicated my life to Jesus and teaching His teachings to others.

Do you want to be more like me?

You can celebrate my feast day with me on April 29th.

I pray for you every day of your life.

St. Catherine of Siena, pray for us!

Copyright:

Clipart: © PentoolPixie © LimeandKiwiDesigns
Licensed purchased: 1/10/2024

About the Author

Abigail Gartland

I love the saints and I love my faith. The idea for sharing the stories of the saints with little ones came when my dear friends were expecting their first baby. I wanted to create something as unique and special as our friendship. Each book is dedicated to very special people and groups who have enriched my faith in different ways. I am blessed to write these stories and appreciate the unending support of my family and friends. When I am not writing, I am a middle school teacher. I hope you enjoy these stories. I pray for each and every person who opens one of my books to learn more about the saints.

Abbie

www.ingramcontent.com/pod-product-compliance
Lightning Source LLC
LaVergne TN
LVHW051042070526
838201LV00067B/4897